First American Edition, 2007
Second American Edition, 2011
Third American Edition, 2015

Published in the United States

Contents

PART 5: SUGGESTED READING..........page 75

PART 6: WEBSITES..........page 83

NOTES

ABOUT THE AUTHOR

INVESTING TO WIN

Introduction

Why another book on investing? Hasn't it all been written before? Do I really have anything new to say?

Of course, a little of this information will be a refresher for you. I also hope you will learn something new, too. We will cover some original ideas like my proprietary tactic called The Free Dividend Cash Flow Strategy. We will also look at various distinctive investments like exchange-traded funds, commodities and special-situation stocks.

Am I qualified to write this book?

What is my experience? Am I licensed to advise others on their investments?

I have been investing my own funds and recommending investments since I was about 20 years old. I have been licensed as a stockbroker, financial advisor and insurance agent simultaneously since the year 2000. I am now professionally managing millions of dollars in assets for dozens of clients in several states. And as for the first question I will let you decide if I am qualified to write this book after you have read through it....

I hope you enjoy this volume...

...find and use a few ideas profitably and send me some feedback. You can find my contact information near the back of the book. Please feel free to get in touch with me regarding ideas, questions, comments or topics you would like covered in future editions of this book.

Necessity of Investing

Is investing necessary? Isn't it risky? What can one expect from setting money aside into various assets?

Those are great questions that I have received from my clients, relatives and investing class participants. We will cover some of the rewards, risks and concepts of investing.

How Important Are Saving and Investing?

According to the US Census in the year 2000, our homes made up 32.3 percent of our average net worth. Another third (33.9 percent) was represented by savings and retirement funds. The remaining third was not retirement funds or liquid, for example, businesses and vehicles.

What Does All of This Mean?

It looks like we need to plan a bit better for retirement and other essential goals.

If you dig a little deeper into the same Census report, you discover that the median value of our retirement funds is roughly $18,645. How long would that last if we were to spend $2,000 a month on expenses? ANSWER: not long enough! It would last UNDER ten months!

What about Social Security?

The last time I read my annual report from the government, it said that Social Security was designed as a SUPPLEMENT, not our main source of retirement funds. It also said that by the year 2042 the system would only be able to fund 73 percent of the benefits promised.

Now, I don't want to sound like a pessimist, but our population is aging AND living longer. That is creating a possibility of under-funding our social contracts. It is ultimately up to us to figure out alternative solutions.

The Eighth Wonder of the World

It is said that Albert Einstein called compounding the eighth wonder of the world. I agree with that completely. Here is an example why.

If you had $1,000 to invest for twenty years and you received SIMPLE interest of eight percent annually, you would wind up with a total of $2,600. That eight percent simple return is pretty decent if you compared it to an imaginary four percent inflation rate, right?

Let's take a look at that inflation rate for a moment. With the same $1,000 for twenty years compounded at four percent, you would need $2,191 to buy the equivalent thousand dollars' worth of consumer goods. Do you see the power of compounding to potentially work AGAINST you? Now let's look at compounding working IN your favor.

Again take $1,000 and <u>compound</u> it at eight percent annually for two decades. You wind up with a very healthy $4,661. That is an extra $2,000 compared to simple interest. And you also outpaced our hypothetical four percent inflation rate WITH CASH TO SPARE.

The magic of compound interest becomes even more exciting when we add monthly cash into the investment. For example, if you added $100 per month to the above funds you would pocket $63,968! You would have contributed only $25,000 total! Keep in mind we are not factoring in taxes or various investment fees.

What Do the Rich Do?

There is more information on accumulating wealth available today than at any other time in history. Again, the US Census sheds some light on wealth accumulation. They found out that the top twenty percent of income earners and the top 5% of wealth gatherers have many habits in common:

- 42.6% own stocks and mutual funds

- 17.5% own their own business or professional practice
- 48.3% invest into an IRA
- 90.2% have cash in the bank

Those are very simple things that almost any of us can do. It does not take much effort to open an IRA account with investment funds or stocks in it. It is easy to deposit money in a bank savings account or CD. Most of us can easily think of and start even a part-time business. All it takes is to do it now. We just need to start with some simple steps and definite plans.

Some Reasons Why the Poor Keep Getting Poorer...

Many times there are good reasons for not getting ahead, ranging from bad luck to health problems. But there are also many differences in habit.

Let's compare the top twenty percent of income earners to the lowest twenty percent of US earners. Of the bottom bracket:

- only 5.6% own stocks or mutual funds
- 5% own a business or profession
- 6.2% contribute to an IRA and
- less then half (40.5%) have cash in the bank

As we can see, there are VERY SPECIFIC things the rich do that others do not. They are willing to invest and risk and create income in different ways other than a job and relying on the government.

The Top Five Percent Have 23 Times More Wealth Than the Bottom Twenty Percent Combined!

What else are they doing differently? They also own their own homes, own and contribute to other retirement accounts like SEP-IRAs and 401Ks, and hold small amounts in depreciating "assets" like vehicles.

As Your Assets Grow so Does Your Income...

According to the same government information, the top five percent of income earners have grown their inflation-adjusted cash flow more than the bottom twenty percent. From 1967 to 2001, the lowest group increased their income by 523 percent. That is not bad, is it? But the upper five per-cent increased their income by almost 700 percent! Both did well, but the people with the LEVERAGE of assets and busi-nesses did best. So increase your assets if you want an ad-vantage in surpassing inflation.

Another way to see this benefit at work is to imagine someone with $1 million in assets. Also imagine this person increases her portfolio at ten percent per year. She would INCREASE her NET WORTH annually by almost twice what the average household <u>makes</u> in a year! This person's assets would increase by $100,000 in one year. And the average family's income is just over $50,000, as of 2013. Do you see the power of assets? I see this very thing happen all of the time with investors.

Also, imagine the same millionaire who earns five percent in income from those assets. She would make a passive income of $50,000 without even touching the principal amount. So there is tremendous leverage and advantage to gain by acquiring and compounding assets.

Basics & Asset Classes

INVESTING TO WIN

What is a Stock?

A stock is a small piece of a business. You will hear the term "public company". That means it is owned by the public. It could be a company worth $200 million dollars and you own two-hundred dollars' worth. But you still own and share in that .000001 percent of the company. That is one of the incredible benefits of living in a free-market economy with a thriving and regulated stock market.

When you own a stock, you own a small portion of the business. If it succeeds, then your stock value <u>may</u> go up. It does NOT guarantee an increase in stock price if the company is doing well financially. Nor does a company losing money month after month mean the stock will fall in value. I will cover reasons and ideas of why that is so, later in the book.

You can earn dividends on a stock, but the company is NOT obligated to pay you a dime. If they do, you can sometimes get large dividends in the range of three to eight percent. Sometimes you can get a larger dividend, but you want to make sure a company is not paying too much of their earnings to you as a dividend. For example, if a company earns one dollar a share annually and they pay out ninety cents per share as a dividend, then that could be too high of a payout. That equals a ninety percent payout and may not be sustainable in the future. That could put your dividend in jeopardy.

How Does One Analyze a Stock?

There are many factors to look at and consider in investigating an individual stock. You can look at volume, price, earnings-per-share, ratios, debt and a lot more. We will look at all of these, but first let's look at the two main ways to think of stock analysis.

The First Way is Technical Analysis

Technical analysis is a way of looking at the supply and demand of a stock, including pricing, volume, chart prices, moving stock price averages and other measures. This way ignores the basic business numbers.

The Second is Fundamental Analysis

This type of examination looks at what technical analysis ignores: business model, earnings, revenues, marketing methods, management experience, growth potential, price-to-earnings ratio, price-to-sales ratio and other "fundamental" numbers and concepts.

Is One Better Than the Other?

I prefer to use both of these methods, relying more on fundamental aspects. Considering all areas of a company and stock is important to help you pick strong enterprises that are selling at healthy share prices.

What is a Business Model?

A business model is the basic method of conducting business for a particular company. An example is Dell Computers. What is their business model? They sell computers direct to consumers and businesses, bypassing the retail channel. What is Office Max's business model? They sell office supplies, including computers, to consumers and businesses using retail stores and having a comprehensive selection of products. What is NBTY's business model? They are a company you have probably not heard of before, but you can understand them quickly by knowing their business model. What is it? They sell vitamins and supplements to consumers via internet sales, direct-order catalogs and toll-free numbers, through retail vitamin stores, previously, through network marketing consumer-to-consumer sales, and to companies through manufacturing and wholesaling.

So you can learn a lot about how a company operates and their potential for success and survival by understanding their basic business model. What company probably has a greater chance of survival in an economic downturn (all other things being equal)? A company that sells a low-priced service that a great number of consumers need monthly or a company that sells a high-priced product that only needs to be replaced every five or more years? I would put my money on the low-priced, monthly-replaced business model.

What is Market Capitalization?

The "market cap", as it is sometimes referred to, is the total value of the company. You simply look at two numbers. The first one is the price per share of the company. The second number is the total "shares outstanding." The "shares out" in the stock market is the number of shares the company has sold to the public. You can very easily find both of these numbers on most financial web sites that analyze companies. You will see two of these sites listed at the back of this book (Reuters and FinViz).

For example, the market cap of a company with a share price of $25 and ten million shares outstanding is $250 million dollars. That is the market capitalization or market value of the company.

Here is the math:

$$\$25 \times 10,000,000 = \$250,000,000 \text{ market cap}$$

What is a Growth Stock?

A growth stock is a company that is rapidly expanding (or expected to expand) their earnings and/or revenues. They also may be expanding their debt for business purposes, too. So this growth does not come without a price.

What is a Value Stock?

A value stock is a company that is selling at a "cheap price." That can mean many things, including a low P/E ratio, a low P/S ratio, a high book value relative to the share price and others.

Value investing is my preferred style because you can pick up stocks that are selling at "discounted" prices. It is like going into the supermarket and finding one of your favorite items on sale that day. In the stock market you can find great sales like these everyday.

What is GARP Stock Investing?

GARP is an acronym for Growth At a Reasonable Price. As you can guess this approach simply combines both growth and value investing. With this method, you are looking at growth companies selling in the market at value prices. A very famous and successful GARP investor was Peter Lynch, for example.

What is a Price-to-Earnings Ratio?

A P/E ratio is just simple math. It is a company's market

value (price) divided by the company's net earnings.

For example, if you have Music Magic Inc. with a total market value (also known as market capitalization) of $100 million and earnings of $10 million, their P/E ratio would be ten.

Let's look at the math:

$100 million price
divided by
$10 million earnings

= 10 P/E

Which is Best: Low- or High-P/E?

In my opinion, the best P/E to look for is a low one. That way you are investing into a company that earns a lot of money relative to the price of the company.

Here is another example. If you had a stock with a P/E of 100 that means they have only one-tenth of the profitability of a stock with a P/E of ten. Assuming the same market capitalization of $500 million the more-profitable company earns $50 million versus the 100 P/E Company earning only $5 million. All other things being equal which company would you rather own a piece of?

What is a Price-to-Sales Ratio?

A P/S ratio is a very vital number to look at. It was created by Kenneth Fisher and popularized in his book, Super Stocks. As he describes, it is helpful for analyzing a company when there are no earnings or irregular earnings. Why? Because revenues (sales) are more consistent than earnings, it is easier to examine a stock even when the company is going through an abnormal time.

But I digress. The price-to-sales ratio is another simple math result. You take the price of a company (their market capitalization) and divide it by their annual sales. Let's say you have a company with a $250 million market "cap" (capitalization) and annual revenues of $1 billion; then the P/S ratio would be .25.

Here is the math:

$250 million divided by $1 billion = .25

Let's say you have another company with a $4 billion market value and annual sales of $1 billion; the P/S is four. You divide $4 billion by $1 billion and you get a P/S of four.

Look For the Low P/S Ratio Stocks...

Similar to the low P/E stocks, I think the lower P/S shares can be potential values versus the possibly over-valued and popular stocks that more people are investing in.

Could the Earnings Yield Be the Best Single Measure of Stock Value?

I think it definitely could be! I consider it to be the **true measure** of how you, as a stockholder, are actually benefiting from the company you invested in. You may not actually receive all of the net earnings in cash, but the company can buy back shares with net income, pay you cash dividends, AND/OR reinvest into the growing enterprise. But, first of all, what is an "earnings yield"? It is the opposite of the P/E ratio. It is essentially the E/P ratio. You divide a companies' total earnings by the total market price of the stock.

For example, if the company you are looking at has annual earnings of $20 million and a market value of $200 million, then the earnings yield would be .10 (expressed as a percentage that would be 10%). So for every dollar
you are investing into the company, it is earning for you ten cents, or ten percent of a dollar.

Why does that matter for finding an undervalued company to invest in or an overvalued company to possibly avoid? Well, let's look at a company to avoid as well as a possible value to research and maybe invest in.

If a wonderful and popular company that everyone adored was making $1 billion dollars every year in net income that <u>looks</u> very good. But if that same business was valued on the stock market for $100 billion would the earnings yield be to low? The earnings yield would be a paltry one percent! So for every dollar YOU INVEST INTO THAT STOCK the company is actually only producing one penny in net income for you, the shareholder and part-owner.

It could be a great company that is well-managed and liked by the public and probably growing. But is it a smart investment?

But let's look at the other viewpoint. Let's say you have a company earning the same $1billion annually and they are priced on the stock market at only $5 billion dollars. That would give you an earnings yield of 20%! Can you see the better value? It bears repeating, in this example, for every dollar invested in this stock, the shareholder receives the benefit from 20 cents in earnings.

As you can tell, because we compare net earnings versus market value, we get a more-accurate measure of value to the shareholder. Because of this, I consider the earnings yield the True Shareholder Net Profit AND the **BEST** measure of stock value.

What is a Bond?

In most cases a bond is a loan to a government or a company. The government can be local, national or international. The company can be based in the US or in a different country.

Unlike a stock that you share ownership in, a bond makes you like the bank. That can be a good thing. Why? Like the bank, you can collect a set interest rate on your money. That institution is OBLIGATED to pay you some kind of interest. They might pay you twice a year, four times a year, monthly or when the bond "matures", or becomes fully payable back to you. For example, let's say you buy a bond for $1,000 for Toyota Corporation and they have a 6.5 percent annual interest rate payable twice a year. You will collect $65 dollars per year in the form of two payments of $32.50.

Whether the price of Toyota stock goes up, down or nowhere at all, you are collecting $65 every single year. Why? You are a bond holder and not a stockholder. Just like the mortgage on a house, they are on the line to pay interest or risk defaulting on their debt. Just like you and I, if they default and have bad credit, it is harder to borrow in the future. If the company or government wants to expand and survive, they will try to maintain a good credit rating.

Are There Other Specific Types of Bonds?

Yes, there are many different bond types and there are new ones emerging periodically.

One type is a zero-coupon bond. This one does NOT pay you interest as you hold it, but at the end of the life of the loan. And you buy the bond at a price lower than the face value. If it is a ten year bond for $1,000, you might pay $700 today and collect the full $1,000 in ten years. The difference of $300 represents the interest due to you. Just like the name says, you get zero interest until the bond matures.

Another type of bond is called a municipal bond. A "muni" bond is a local government bond like an airport, hospital or toll-road. When you buy an individual municipal bond, you will get two payments per year so long as it is not a zero-coupon bond. These payments will be exempt from federal taxation. Yes, you did read that correctly. The income is free from federal taxation. It can get better, too. If the bond you buy is based in the state you live in, it will be exempt from state tax as well. That is known as "double-exempt." And if that was not enough there are "triple-exempt" bonds, if you lived in a city that taxed your income (like New York City).

Some More Types of Bonds

There are even more types of bonds available. And by the time you read this book, there may even be a newer bond. You just have to keep checking the pulse of the financial markets because there are innovations occurring regularly.

You may have heard of international bonds. These are, typically, corporate or government bonds of developed countries (larger, steady and more mature economies like Japan, Germany and the UK).

There are also emerging market bonds. These are also corporate and government bonds, but they are from newly emerging economies like South America, China and Russia. These are more aggressive investments due to their lack of political and/or economic stability. Because there is more risk involved, they will usually pay you more interest on the bonds.

Another type of bond is a convertible bond. No, these are not necessarily more comfortable in the summer. These are corporate bonds that can be "converted" into common stock in the future at a specified dollar price. So you can get a current income stream from the bonds, and if the stock goes up significantly in value, then you can convert it to the stock for a potential increase in value.

With this type of bond you can get the best of both worlds. You can get the stability and obligation of a bond PLUS the upside appreciation potential of a stock. You do usually pay for this feature: the issuer will probably give a lower annual interest rate on the bond AND the stock will almost certainly have to rise to a higher level than where it currently is before you can <u>profitably</u> convert it to the common stock.

These are not all the types of bonds available, but they are the main breeds you are likely to encounter.

How Do I Analyze Bonds and Bond Mutual Funds?

Fortunately, there is a cut-and-dry way of looking at the health of a bond or bond fund. Again, similar to having a personal credit score, there are credit scores for institutions that issue bonds. Instead of a number, they use letters. There are several companies that rate bond issuers. We will look at the ratings for two prominent services: Standard & Poor's (S&P) and Moody's Investor Services (Moody's). We are going to divide the list in half, split between investment grade and speculative. I will cover the differences in a moment.

Investment Grade

S&P   Moody's

AAA   Aaa
AA+   Aa1, Aa2, Aa3
AA, AA-   A1, A2, A3
A+, A, A-   Baa1, Baa2
BBB+, BBB   Baa3
BBB-

Speculative Grade

S&P   Moody's

BB+, BB   Ba1, Ba2, Ba3
BB-   B1, B2, B3
B+, B, B-   Caa
CCC+, CCC   Ca
CCC-, CC   C
C
D

What Do All of These Letters and Numbers Mean?

So, essentially, the top half of these grades is a more-conservative risk. And the bottom half is more high-risk. Typically, the more risk you take on with bonds and these ratings, the higher annual interest you will earn. Also, the "high-yields" have a higher chance of default. So do your research before putting money at stake.

What is a Mutual Fund?

A mutual fund is a cluster of investors pooling their money together to be managed by a professional investor, the mutual fund sponsor. They can invest in most asset classes like stocks, bonds, real estate, foreign currencies, commodities and others. They can have various strategies like special situations, large companies or international bonds, for example.

The mutual fund sponsor will have an annual management fee. This covers day-to-day management of the pooled funds, including trading costs, management compensation, marketing expenses and other commonplace costs.

You should read the mutual fund prospectus very carefully. This is usually a plain-looking black-and-white document that describes the fund objectives, managers and their experience and many other important points. But particularly important to read is the fee details. Here you will see hypothetical examples of annual expenses.

What are A, B, C and No-Load Shares?

These are the four main classes of mutual funds. These descriptions indicate the fees involved for sales and management of the funds. You could have one mutual fund called Variety Fund, for example, that has an A, B and C share. Then the same Variety Fund could also have a no-load version, too.

Before we get too involved with the differences between these share classes, you should realize that there are hundreds of mutual fund companies and they all have different policies, fees and sales charges. And they can change very quickly. So you really need to talk with someone about these fine points before committing your money.

The A shares have an up-front sales charge for the purchase of the investment in the 4.5 to 5.5 percent range. The annual management fee will normally be significantly lower than the B and C shares. So if you invested $100 dollars, you would actually purchase about $94.50 worth of the fund. This is due to the up-front sales charge. But long-term, you could save on the annual management fee versus the B and C shares. You could save more than one percent per year. This would essentially earn back your fee within about six years. This is most appropriate for a long-term holder of the mutual fund (which is what you want to be anyway). Also, for higher dollar amounts invested, the sales fee may lower. Check with the fund company for complete details.

The B share does not charge you an up-front sales charge. If you invest $100 into the fund, then you will have purchased $100 of the fund shares. But the B share has a higher annual management fee. Again, it could run higher than one percent versus the A share.

Another very important point is that if you completely leave the mutual fund company, you MIGHT be subject to a back-end fee with the B share. This back-end charge can range in years from four to six or more years. For example, if you had a back-end fee that lasted five years the "schedule" might look like this: 5%, 4%, 3%, 2%, 1% then 0%. So if you left the company within the first year, they would charge you five percent. If you left in the second year you would get a charge of four percent and so on until AFTER five years. The good news is after the schedule ends; you can normally completely exit the company and have no other sales charge to account for. And usually, the B share converts into an A share after about eight years. Why is that good? Because you would be paying a much smaller annual management fee compared to the B share.

Are You Hanging in There?

I know that is a lot of information, but it is very important to understand these small differences. These tiny points could save you OR cost you a lot. Are you ready for the next two classes?

I consider the C share a hybrid of sorts between the A and B shares. Some companies let you invest with no up-front charge and some may charge you one percent for the initial sales fee. So that resembles both the A and

B shares. Also, the C share will usually have a back-end charge for one to two years. The company may charge you one to two percent if you completely exit the fund management family. The annual management fee is usually the same or similar to the B share, that is, higher than the A share. So, the C class shares qualities of BOTH the A and B funds.

Now we have the no-load shares. These have no up-front sales charge and usually require that you stay within the fund family for up to 90 days. After this time, you can exit the management company with no back-end or front-end sales fee. The annual management expenses can range from a fraction of a percent to over two percent per year.

"Where Do I Get These Funds?"

Usually you get the A, B and C shares from some kind of broker or adviser at a bank, insurance company, brokerage house or from a mutual fund company. Normally, they are licensed to give you advice on selecting your funds and will, therefore, assist you with ideas.

The no-loads are, more often than not, exclusively from

the mutual fund management company. They may have ads on the internet, TV or other media. They are selling directly to you and are offering you NO ADVICE. You have to select the appropriate funds yourself.

What is an Open-End Mutual Fund?

An open-end mutual fund is a fund that continually issues new shares in their fund as new investment dollars come into the fund pool. Most of the funds you will find in company-sponsored retirement plans will be open-ended. Also, by definition, no-load funds are open-end funds because you invest directly with the mutual fund company and not with a broker through a stock exchange. They are sold at their NAV (net asset value) minus any applicable sales charges.

What is a Closed-End Mutual Fund?

A closed-end fund goes by several names including exchange-traded funds (ETFs). No matter what name is used, the characteristics are the same. They have a fixed number of shares outstanding and can only be purchased on a stock exchange (hence the other name of "exchange-traded fund"); you have to go through either a discount, full-service or other kind of broker to invest in these (although now some are available in annuities and corporate retirement plans), and they can sell at, below OR above their NAV (their underlying value if liquidated of their individual investment holdings).

So there you can see one possible benefit to using closed -end funds: you can buy them "on sale." In other words, if the NAV of a particular fund is $10 per share and you can purchase it for $7 per share, then you are investing "at a discount."

What Do Mutual Funds Invest In?

They can invest in bonds, stocks, real estate, commodities, gold, oil, international stocks, international bonds, international real estate, dividend-paying stocks, growth stocks, currencies, municipal bonds, combinations of the above and much more. There are new categories of mutual funds being created regularly. They even invest into certain sectors of the economy like financials, utilities, technology and on and on.

What Is The Difference Between a Global and an International Mutual Fund?

This is an important question. I talk to people a lot that think the two are the same. And by the name they do sound just alike. But there is a big difference, especially when you are trying to properly diversify your assets. In a nutshell, when you see the name global in the mutual fund name or description, those funds will invest in international AND American (domestic) stocks. The international funds should have NO domestic shares.

So you might _think_ The Global ABC Fund is investing all of your money out of the country. But they could have fifty percent of the assets in large-capitalization US companies. So are you really as diversified as you thought by looking at the name?

On the flip side, if you invested in The International ABC Fund, then 100% of your money should be in foreign shares. Then you can rest assured that you have fully diversified OUTSIDE of the US. Then you can also invest other moneys into domestic funds or shares.

What Is An Annuity?

An annuity is similar to a mutual fund and/or fixed income investment combined with a retirement plan, but it also has life insurance attached to it. It is both an investment security AND an insurance product. They can be very complex. Sometimes you can talk to a stockbroker, advisor or insurance agent, and <u>THEY</u> are confused by the small differences in annuity policies! That is because there are hundreds of different companies offering them, and they ALL have varying policy details. But we will cover the basics of how annuities work, giving you a general guideline on how they work. But REMEMBER: read the fine print of an annuity, especially regarding the various fees.

There Are Two Main Types of Annuities...

The first type we will cover is called a "fixed" annuity. These are the simplest. They offer you a fixed rate of return for a set number of years. For example, you might get a 6% fixed annual return for five years. So in that respect, it is similar to a fixed-income investment like a CD or bond. The insurance company and investment management company helping them will normally have an annual fee. And you usually will need to stay with that annuity company for the five years or risk an exit fee. So the fee structure is similar to a mutual fund.

The Second Main Type of Annuity...

...is called a "variable" annuity. This type of contract is normally invested into a mutual fund or group of mutual funds referred to as "sub-accounts". The returns will vary from day to day and year to year, hence "variable" annuity.

What Is a Surrender Period?

A surrender period is simply the amount of time you, as the annuity contract owner, are agreeing to hold onto the policy. Usually, if you exit the contract too soon, you will be subject to a stiff penalty. I have seen them as high as ten percent! When the surrender charges are this high, you are probably looking at a company to run away from quickly. But most reputable firms start the penalty at maybe 8% and then every year or two you hold onto the contract, the penalty goes down. Eventually, at the end of the contract, the charge will disappear entirely. Keep in mind, all companies are different, and so the length of the surrender period could be three years or seven years or four years. My point is: find out first before you invest.

What Is An M&E Charge?

M&E stands for "mortality and expense". This is where the insurance comes in. All annuities have a death benefit or insurance benefit tied to the investment. If you were the "annuitant" on the contract and you invested $10,000 into your fixed annuity and then you passed away, then your beneficiaries would receive this death benefit.

What Is An Administrative Charge?

The "admin" charge is a small annual fee assessed by the annuity company for, you guessed it, administering the paperwork, quarterly statements, postage charges and other activities necessary to running the investment for you. Usually, this fee is on all types of annuities and costs well under half a percent per year. But it does vary company to company and contract to contract. You should always ask exactly what this fee costs. If the admin is <u>over</u> .25% (one-fourth of a percent) annually, seriously reconsider this contract AND company.

Are There Additional Fees With a Variable Annuity?

There are added annual fees that are used to compensate the money managers. They can range from under one percent to over two percent. You should check with the company BEFORE you invest.

Why Are Annuities Similar to Retirement Plans?

They are similar to qualified retirement plans because the gains on the underlying investments are tax-deferred until you pull them out. When you pull out the gains, then you will be taxed at that time. Also, if you pull out the investment before you are age 59 ½, then normally, you will be subject to a non-refundable 10% penalty courtesy of the government. Of course, after that age, then you will not have a penalty from the government (but you may be subject to a surrender-charge penalty from the annuity company—I said they can be confusing, didn't I?!).

Why Are Annuities Similar to Pension Plans?

You normally have the option of "annuitizing" your annuity contract if you desire. What this means is that you will receive a stream of income based on the value of your contract. The insurance company will have different payout options for you to choose from. For example, "period-certain" means you and/or your beneficiaries will receive a regular check for a definite number of years, possibly 10 or 20 years.

What Is a REIT?

A REIT is a real estate investment trust. It is a company that buys, manages and sometimes sells individual pieces of real estate. Usually, they are buying the properties, holding for possible appreciation and collecting a cash flow from the underlying real estate. By law, to be structured as a REIT, they must pay out 95 percent or more of their taxable income as a dividend to the shareholders. For this reason, you will usually find these investments paying a high yield.

REITs can invest in malls, apartments, mortgages, warehouses, retail, international assets and other types of property. Most will normally specialize in one of these types although some will combine various styles of property into one company.

REITs are listed on a stock exchange and can be arranged into a mutual fund that owns many different trusts.

What Is a Commodity?

A commodity is a natural resource like oil, natural gas, coal, water, oranges, sugar, cocoa, wheat, cattle...you get the idea. They can be very sought-after and valuable like oil or common like water. But you can invest in these through mutual funds and diversify your portfolio and potentially profit. You should refer to the asset allocation portion of this book and see what suggested percentage of your assets might be appropriate for a commodities fund.

There are now several commodity-based mutual funds. These can be a more conservative way to invest into this asset class, producing added diversification from stocks and bonds.

Returns

Have Realistic Expectations

We all get a wake-up call when historic events shake the financial markets. From The Great Depression of the 1930s, to the big one-day crash in 1987 and then the three year stock market drop from 2000-2002, and even the historically low rates of interest in the latest market tumble, these all serve as reminders of how the markets can move.

This is why we want to take a look at average returns and NOT get petrified by extreme returns. Similar events will probably rock the worldwide markets many times again. The key is to maintain an historic perspective and not a fearful outlook.

What Do Stocks and Bonds Return?

With investing, there are very few sure things. But we can look back through history to get an idea of how some of these assets have performed in the past. Below is a sample of annual returns, from 1926-2014, according to Ibbotson Associates, Inc.

Small Companies	12.2%
Large Companies	10.1
Government Bonds	5.7
U.S. Treasury Bills	3.5
Inflation	2.9

These are average annual returns. There is no guarantee that they will perform the same in the future. Although from year to year the returns can be negative or positive, I would have been very happy with these results for my portfolio.

After we take compounding interest into mind, these COMMON returns become anything but average! If you had invested $10,000 and earned ten percent for twenty years, through the power of compounding interest and dividends, you would have $73,281. That is equivalent to OVER 31% simple interest yearly! You probably won't be getting that at the bank too soon. That is the power of reinvesting dividends, interest and capital gains. This also is not factoring in taxes, investment/trading fees and other costs.

Strategies

#1: Dollar-Cost Averaging

What is Dollar-Cost Averaging?

This is one of the oldest and most-effective strategies known to aid you in building wealth. It has been endorsed by dozens of financial experts; chief among them was Benjamin Graham. This mentor of Warren Buffett wrote about dollar-cost averaging (DCA) in his famous book called <u>The Intelligent Investor.</u>

The technique is very simple. An example is if you had $100 taken from your checking account and automatically deposited each month into a stock mutual fund that would be dollar-cost averaging. You are simply investing a fixed dollar amount on a regular basis. It could be any dollar amount, any regular interval and most any investment. But the most common is investing monthly, as in the case of a retirement plan at work.

Why does it Work?

DCA works for several reasons. It takes the emotion out of investing. Instead of worrying about the economy or the markets or hundreds of other minute financial details, you simply INVEST. You don't think, but you take action. Also, when the market is low, you accumulate more shares. When the market is overvalued, you buy less overpriced shares because you are putting in a FIXED dollar amount.

Here is a comparison based on a flat market:

Month:	Share Price:	DCA:
January	$10	10 shares @ $100
February	$9	11.11 shares @ $100
March	$8.25	12.12 shares @ $100
April	$7.50	13.33 shares @ $100
May	$8.75	11.43 shares @ $100

June	$9	11.11 shares @ $100
July	$10.75	9.3 shares @ $100
August	$11	9.09 shares @ $100
September	$10.25	9.76 shares @ $100
October	$8.25	12.12 shares @ $100
November	$8	12.5 shares @ $100
December	$10	10 shares @ $100

<u>Here are the results:</u>

One-time investment, number of shares and value: 120 shares @ $1,200 in January and December.

Dollar-cost averaging, number of shares and value: 131.87 shares @ $1,318.70.

Now you can see why this is a highly recommended investment strategy. Even in a flat market where the beginning and end value per share was ten dollars, you could have profited with DCA. By investing a lump sum, you would have had only your initial money. And notice that the price went BOTH above and below ten dollars per share. It is this volatility that can pay off for the long-term, dollar-cost averaging investor.

When the mutual fund price dropped to its low of seven and a half dollars, you didn't get scared and sell out. By STICKING TO YOUR STRATEGY, you took the emotion out of investing. You ignored the market news and stuck to what works. This is why stock market volatility is your friend.

#2: Asset Allocation

What Is Asset Allocation?

Asset allocation is simply investing into a "basket" of different asset classes all at once. The asset classes I use below are cash and cash equivalents, bonds, stocks, real estate, commodities and options. You can also include foreign currencies, hedge funds, private equity and others.

Does Asset Allocation Really Work?

It can help out your portfolio in several ways. Although there are no guarantees, asset allocation CAN reduce overall portfolio risk, provide more-consistent returns compared to investing in just one asset class, and keep an investor disciplined rather than chasing "hot" investments.

Because investments "behave" differently at different times, owning a broad mix of assets lets you capture the returns of ALL of the best-performing asset classes. By annually selling some of the investments that have gained in value and reinvesting into the assets that have dropped in value, you are taking money out of the "hot" investments (this is called "rebalancing").   This way, you are <u>systematically</u> "buying low and selling high."

A Short Questionnaire…

Here is a helpful and short questionnaire that can assist you with allocating most of your investments. It will help you analyze company retirement plans, IRAs, brokerage accounts, real estate investments and other holdings you may have.

How to Do It

All you have to do is simply circle your answer to the questions, total the points and look at your appropriate asset allocation. You may want to answer these questions from time to time, possibly every one to two years. This will keep your investment portfolio updated based on the changes in your life. Here we go.

A.   When do you plan on using these funds?

0-1 year...4 points
2-5 years...6 points
6-10 years...12 points
11-19 years...14 points
20+ years...20 points

B.   What is your age?

35 or younger...20 points
36-50 years...12 points
51-65 years...6 points
66 and older...4 points

C.   What is your liquid net worth (e.g. stocks, bonds, mutual funds, cash, money markets, CDs, annuities, etc.)?

Less than or equal to $25,000...2 points
$25,001-$50,000...4 points
$50,001-$99,999...6 points
$100,000-$250,000...8 points
$251,000-$1,000,000...10 points
Over $1,000,000...18 points

D.   Add the following points for each asset that you have invested in for over one year:

Stocks...10 points
Bonds...10 points
Mutual funds...5 points
Options (e.g. puts and calls)...12 points

E.   How long have you invested?

Less than one year...2 points
1-5 years...4 points
6-10 years...5 points
Over ten years...6 points

Total Points: _____

12-35 Points = Conservative Allocation
36-58 Points = Moderate Allocation
59-81 Points = Moderate Growth Allocation
82-101 Points = Growth Allocation

*   *   *

The following pages contain the four asset allocations, along with a pie-chart, to visually show you the various asset types to use for your investing program.

CONSERVATIVE ALLOCATION: **70% Fixed Income**
                                   30% Growth

CONSERVATIVE ALLOCATION

- Cash, CDs* 15%

- Short-term US bonds 15%

- Long-term US bonds 30%

- International bonds 10%

- Small/Mid- sized stocks 5%

- Large value stocks 15%

- International stocks 5%

- Real Estate stocks 5%

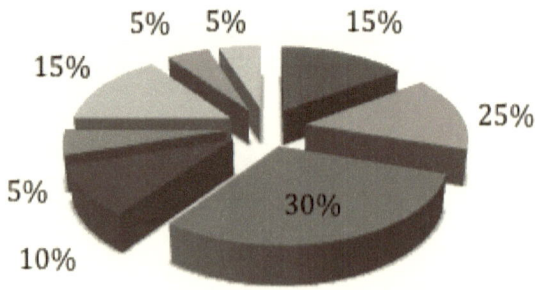

MODERATE ALLOCATION: **50% Fixed Income**
                                        50% Growth

MODERATE ALLOCATION

- Cash, CDs* 10%
- Short-term US bonds 10%
- Long-term US bonds 20%
- International bonds 10%
- Small/Mid- sized stocks 5%
- Large value stocks 25%
- Large growth stocks 10%
- International stocks 5%
- Real Estate stocks 5%

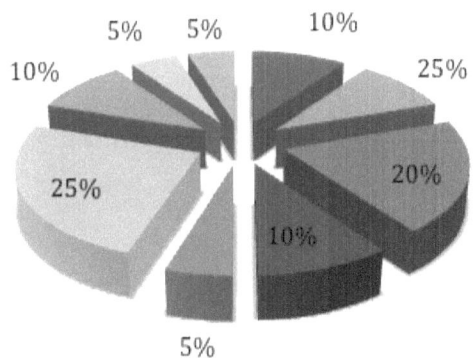

MODERATE GROWTH ALLOCATION: **25% Fixed Income**
75% Growth

MODERATE GROWTH

- Cash, CDs* 7%
- Short-term US bonds 3%
- Long-term US bonds 10%
- International bonds 5%
- Small/Mid- sized stocks 20%
- Large value stocks 15 %
- Large growth stocks 15 %
- International stocks 15%
- Real Estate stocks 5%
- Commodity funds 5%

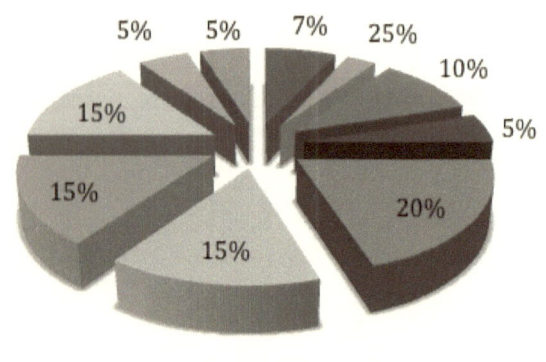

GROWTH ALLOCATION: **15% Fixed Income**
85% Growth

GROWTH ALLOCATION

- Cash, CDs* 5%
- Long-term US bonds 5%
- International bonds 5%
- Small/Mid- sized stocks 20%
- Large value stocks 10%
- Large growth stocks 15%
- International stocks 20%
- Micro-cap stocks 5%
- Real Estate stocks 5%
- Commodity funds 5%
- Options funds** 5%

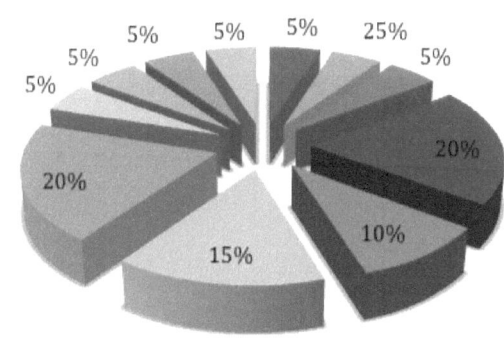

A Few Explanations...

*Short-term CDs, maturing in one year or less.

**Options funds are relatively new closed-end funds that usually invest in a stock index. They sell call stock options that generate income (in addition to any dividends) from the portfolio. Sometimes these options funds can yield in the area of 7-10% annually.

*   *   *

These are general guidelines on percentages to invest. They are NOT absolute recommendations. You should use these to <u>start</u> your allocation process and adjust the portions based on how you feel about risk and your individual needs.

The nice thing about these allocations is that you can use them as a guide for most of your investments. If you have IRAs, work retirement plans, whole-life insurance policies or annuities, or regular brokerage and mutual fund accounts, you can use this allocation as a vehicle that steers you into your desired overall allocation.

#3: Special Situation Small-Cap Stock

What is a "Special Situation Small-Cap Stock"?

Let's start off with small-cap stock. Small-cap stands for small-capitalization. Very simply, this is a small company. They have a small capitalization in the stock market. This is not the big company you see in practically every sizable town throughout the US or the world. These could be significant operations that you just may have never heard of before. They might be selling hundreds of millions of dollars in revenue per year but they are simply smaller and less well known than world-wide brands.

Special situation stocks are a little harder to define and understand. In general, they are companies that are going through changes. They could be entering or exiting bankruptcy or having legal problems or other "special situations" that set them apart from the average company. As you can see, the definition is broad and general. There are even hedge funds that devote their whole portfolio to only special situation companies. It can be very rewarding and very risky, too.

Both of these types of stocks are "stand alone" investments. You could have a small-cap stock that is NOT a special situation. And you could have a large-capitalization company that is a special situation.

Let's Combine the Two

Identifying both separately can lead to investment opportunities. Finding the two together can result in a complete investment strategy. For example, in about the year 2002, I noticed a very well-known company with a lot of revenue that was having legal problems (the special situation). Their stock price plummeted, and they were now a small-cap stock. I recommended it to a client at a little over $4 per share. After about three years, the company rose in value to $98.

This is just an example of the POTENTIAL return. This same company also declared bankruptcy and reemerged successfully, which is often perilous and rare. So there is quite a bit of risk involved. On the flipside, another company that I had personally invested in went from over seven dollars per share to under fifty cents within one year. So you must be aware of the risks involved.

#4: Free-Dividend Cash Flow Strategy

The Strategy Explained...

The Free Dividend Cash Flow Strategy (FDCS) © Ronald S. Phillips is a proprietary tactic that I invented as a means to minimize risk, create income and have a disciplined sell-strategy for individual stock investing.

Let me give you an example and you will see all of these attributes working together. In the early 2000's, JP Morgan Bank was selling at a very low price, in the low $20's. They were also yielding (paying an annual dividend equal to) seven percent per year! This was the nation's second largest bank at the time, paying a better income than a one-year CD! They were also a healthy company according to their balance sheet.

So I recommended this stock to a client for his portfolio. It was great timing. Within a few years, the stock doubled. So with the FDCS, you would sell half of your stock when it doubles. You are essentially getting all of the money you initially invested back into your hands, resting safely in a money market account. It could take a few months or years and years for it to double. It doesn't matter. The selling is the same. Sell whenever it doubles.

The second main part of this plan is to buy companies paying a sizeable dividend. This way, when you sell half of your position, the other half is paying you an income. I call this a "free" dividend because you have taken your original money out of the stock and have ZERO risk to your original investment.

Let's take a look at this example with dollars involved.

Let's say your original investment was $1,000 into JP Morgan (the ticker for JP Morgan was JPM). This is what it would like:

$1,000 into JPM @7% yield = $1,000 in shares & $70 annual dividend

THEN: JPM doubles & sell half = $1,000 cash & $1,000 JPM stock with $35 yearly income

This example looks a lot better when you add another zero or two. Three and a half percent may look small but you now have ALL of your starting investment out. Then there is the possibility that the remaining stock can go up in value even more. And, if the company continues to grow, then they may increase your dividend income more in the future.

#5: The 3-Step, No-Brainer Mutual Fund Strategy

The 3-Step, No-Brainer Mutual Fund Strategy

This is a tactic that is very simple and can be used as a stand-alone approach. It is very simple and easy to manage. If this is your only investment it can pay off handsomely for you if allowed to work as described.

STEP ONE: Invest in a Balanced Mutual Fund or Asset Allocation Fund

A balanced fund is a combination of assets. It is usually a blend of stocks, bonds and cash. You might see the word "balanced" in the name of the fund. For example, it could be called "Dreydelity Balanced Fund".

It could even include international stocks and bonds, real estate or other types of investments. And therefore could be an asset allocation fund. Both types will work.

But the key is to have the diversification of various asset classes. This will provide a one-stop investment for the long haul that can be held for years with minimal maintenance.

STEP TWO: Dollar-Cost Average into the Fund & Invest More as it Drops in Value

As you learned earlier, you will accumulate more shares or less-expensive shares with the DCA strategy as the price of the shares move in value. And when the price drops significantly, as in a "bear" market, you add EVEN MORE than the usual amount. By doing that, you are making market volatility work FOR YOU.

STEP THREE: Invest for Fifteen or More Years

Why fifteen years? According to Morningstar Direct, from the years 1926-2014, you would have had a 99.8% chance of profit if you had invested in stocks and held for fifteen or more years. Yes, you read that correctly; you would have been virtually ASSURED a positive return.

This time frame factors in many HUGE events like The Great Depression, Pearl Harbor bombing, JFK assassination, many recessions, high interest rates, the dot-com bubble, the Global Financial Crisis and much more.

With that knowledge, you can now see how erroneous it is when someone equates the stock market with gambling. I would much rather have those odds than a Vegas slot machine.

For the same time period, if you had held for ten years, you would have had a 94.4% chance of a positive return. So that is a very good chance as well. But I recommend holding for fifteen or more years.

Suggested Reading

Why an Entire Section?

This last part of the book is so important that I gave it its own section. This will really help you to further understand investing and fill in any spots I have missed.

Where do I Start?

I will list these books from easy to moderate to advanced books. Then you can start where you feel comfortable and confident. If you are fairly advanced, you may still want to review some of the basics in the easier books. After all, like most things in life, investing is built on the foundation of basics.

EASY:

The Richest Man in Babylon by George S. Clason

This is a wonderfully simple book to read. It was recommended to me by my dad as the most important book he thought I should read. And it turns out to be the best one I have found to introduce one to investing. Once you have read it you will see that it makes a great gift for younger people to show them the importance of saving and investing.

It is written as a story set in ancient Babylon. Here, the main character learns "The Five Laws of Gold." And because it is a story you discover the lessons without realizing you are learning.

Rich Dad, Poor Dad by Robert T. Kiyosaki and Sharon L. Lechter, C.P.A.

This was an instant classic the moment it hit the bookshelf. The authors bring home some powerful concepts in an easy-to-understand manner. They discuss why your home is a liability INSTEAD of an asset (because it causes cash to flow OUT of your pocket); they redefine assets and liabilities, and they very simply describe and illustrate the concepts of the personal balance sheet and money movement. It is a very groundbreaking book. I recommend all of his and his advisors' books as well.

Think Like a Billionaire by Donald Trump

Mr. Trump has written many great books. He certainly has the "fruit on the tree", displaying, by his accomplishments, that he is very qualified to write financial books. This is his most balanced book, covering real estate, cash management, stocks, public relations and much more. It really is a financial planning book in disguise. I would recommend all of his writing in addition to this book.

MODERATE:

The Millionaire Next Door by Thomas J. Stanley and William D. Danko

This is probably my favorite book on investing and wealth. It will really open your eyes when it comes to revealing the "secrets of America's wealthy." The authors studied actual millionaire lifestyles of hundreds and hundreds of wealthy in the US. They came away with seven factors that led to millionaire status.

One of my favorite quotes from this book is "To build wealth, minimize your realized (taxable) income and maximize your unrealized income (wealth/capital appreciation without a cash flow)." It is very relevant to investing. And I came up with a list of investments and strategies that I believe follow this principle. Here they are:

⇒ stocks with no- or low-dividends
⇒ investments in tax-deferred accounts like IRAs, SEP-IRAs and annuities
⇒ tax-efficient mutual funds like index funds and exchange-traded funds
⇒ municipal bonds and municipal bond funds
⇒ raw land
⇒ collectibles and antiques
⇒ privately-held businesses
⇒ a creative accountant
⇒ selling your investments with gains after one year to take advantage of hopefully smaller capital gains taxes
⇒ others you can think of:

_____
_____
_____
_____
_____

ADVANCED:

The 60-Second Investor by Charles Carlson

Mr. Carlson is a successful investor and has distilled some of his knowledge into bite-size pieces that are just a few pages long. He covers some technical topics like price-to-sales ratios, price-to-earnings ratios and other investment analysis ideas. The book introduces many such topics but does it briefly, making this easier to read and understand. Although he does cover many basic ideas, he discusses quite a few advanced topics, making this a more complex book at times.

The Intelligent Investor by Benjamin Graham

This is by far the most advanced book I will mention. The author and the book were both very large influences on the great Warren Buffett. It is probably the most-influential book mentioned by other very sophisticated and successful investors, too. It covers some obscure companies like railroads, but the lessons are applicable today, teaching us about balance sheets and financially healthy companies. He also covers some very good basics like dollar-cost averaging, how mutual funds operate, and asset allocation (primarily including both bond and stock exposure into your portfolio).

Multiple Streams of Income by Robert Allen

This is my favorite money book covering investing, personal finance AND business in one volume. The author popularized the real estate "nothing down" philosophy and includes several real estate topics in his ten streams of income. He also covers stocks, mutual funds, stock options, tax liens, internet businesses, marketing, legal entities, estate planning and pretty much everything else except the kitchen sink.

Websites

Useful Websites for Analyzing Different Asset Classes and Projecting Your Portfolio Value...

Reuters.com

This is a very helpful site for looking up details on stocks. You just type in a stock symbol and then look to the left column for several great categories of stock characteristics like balance sheets, company descriptions and others.

InvestingInBonds.com

This is a great source to get basic, easy-to-understand information on over ten different types of bonds. It covers municipal bonds to government bonds and more.

FinViz.com

Already a very well-known web site, this one offers a free stock screener. The method of downloading this free tool changes so look around the top area for the Stock Screener. This will allow you to input various searches based on company size, P/E ratio, current ratio and dozens of other variables.

As an example of a stock screener, I inputted a screener for stocks with a P/E ratio of fourteen or less; a P/S ratio of half a percent or less, and a minimum dividend yield of three percent. It screened a total of 4,097 issues down to just twenty stocks. So it does an impressive job for a free service. I have found some real winners this way.

CEFconnect.com

This is a good site to look up closed-end mutual funds. You can screen through various asset classes like fixed-income, global, preferred shares, REITs, etc.

Morningstar.com

This company is very well-known for their expert and unbiased mutual fund analysis. Their site is very comprehensive on most information you need on open-end mutual funds. You can look at total annual expenses, management experience and tenure, examples of growth of $10,000 and a lot more. As of this writing, they had both a free version, that is broad in scope, and a premium (paid) version with added information.

MoneyChimp.com

This is a goofy name but a good site for their free financial calculators. You can figure percentage-growth, lump-sum and/or systematic contributions to an investment, years invested and others. With that input, you can see what a certain investment amount would grow to in the future. You can figure what specific dollar amount to invest each month to reach a goal like $100,000. Just click on "calculators" and you can play around with the various scenarios for each cal-culator.

Investopedia.com

This is THE MOST COMPREHENSIVE investing site I have ever visited. I like it for the "dictionary" section. There are hun-dreds and hundreds of definitions regarding mutual funds, stocks, bonds, taxes, real estate and other subjects. They also have articles, tutorials, stock quotes and an interesting stock "simulator." This site really has everything, including the kitchen sink. When I searched the site for "kitchen sink" it responded with an article "Cheap Home Renovations That Pay Off." This is my go-to source when I'm stumped.

Notes:

Notes:

Notes:

Notes:

Notes:

Investor Advantage

NEWSLETTER

PROBLEM:

So many potential investments.

SOLUTION:

> Research less > Learn more > Make money >

…subscribe to **Investor Advantage Newsletter**.

With your subscription **YOU GET:**

⇒ Accurate and unbiased stock analysis

⇒ Timely opportunities

⇒ Unique ideas NOT usually covered by Wall Street and much more

--ABOUT THE AUTHOR--

Ronald Phillips was born and raised in Pueblo, Colorado. He graduated from Central High School and attended what was then the University of Southern Colorado. He has been advising clients on their investments since the year 2000. He currently manages several million dollars in assets for dozens of clients throughout the United States. He is an author of several books, a respected financial columnist & a teacher of investing.

THE AUTHOR CAN BE CONTACTED AT:

2099 W. US Hwy 50 #130-C
Pueblo, CO 81008

(719) 545-6442
RonPhillipsAdvisor@gmail.com